for Advent and the Christmas Season 2021–22

SACRED SPACE

November 28, 2021 to January 8, 2022

from the website www.sacredspace.ie

Prayer from the Irish Jesuits

LOYOLA PRESS.
A JESUIT MINISTRY
Chicago

LOYOLA PRESS.
A JESUIT MINISTRY

3441 N. Ashland Avenue
Chicago, Illinois 60657
(800) 621-1008
www.loyolapress.com

This edition of *Sacred Space for Advent* is published by arrangement with Messenger Publications, 37 Lower Leeson Street, Dublin D02 W938, Ireland.

Loyola Press in Chicago thanks the Irish Jesuits and Messenger Press for preparing this book for publication.

Cover art credit: Shutterstock/pluie_r.

ISBN-13: 978-0-8294-5095-8

Printed in the United States of America.
21 22 23 24 25 Versa 10 9 8 7 6 5 4 3 2 1

Contents

Sacred Space Prayer

Bless all who worship you, almighty God,
from the rising of the sun to its setting:
from your goodness enrich us,
by your love inspire us,
by your Spirit guide us,
by your power protect us,
in your mercy receive us,
now and always.

How to Use This Booklet

During each week of the liturgical year, begin by reading the section entitled 'Something to think and pray about each day this week'. Then proceed through 'The Presence of God', 'Freedom' and 'Consciousness' steps to prepare yourself to hear the word of God in your heart. In the next step, 'The Word', turn to the Scripture reading for each day of the week. Inspiration points are provided in case you need them. Then return to the 'Conversation' and 'Conclusion' steps. Use this process every day of the year.

The Advent retreat at the back of this book follows a similar structure: an invitation to experience stillness, a Scripture passage and reflection points, and suggestions for prayer; you may find it useful to move back and forth between the daily reflections and the retreat.

The First Week of Advent

28 November–4 December 2021

Something to think and pray about each day this week:

For us, in this Advent season, we are being called to realise that the tidy soul, like the tidy house, has to be worked at. It doesn't just happen. If we truly want the Lord to come and stay a while, we have to prepare the way. It's about putting the house in order–the soul in order. Somewhere and somehow we need to hear the centurion's words again and realise his words are ours too: 'Lord, I am not worthy to have you under my roof'.

For that, we need a plan of action, a road map of sorts, to guide us on the journey.

The Sacrament of Reconciliation supplies some of that road map. Its coordinates are already there for us, and the initial movement might be found in 'Bless me Father, for I have sinned'.

Vincent Sherlock, *Let Advent Be Advent*

The Presence of God

'Be still, and know that I am God!' Lord, your words lead us to the calmness and greatness of your presence.

Freedom

God is not foreign to my freedom. The Spirit breathes life into my most intimate desires, gently nudging me towards all that is good. I ask for the grace to let myself be enfolded by the Spirit.

Consciousness

Where do I sense hope, encouragement and growth in my life? By looking back over the past few months, I may see which activities and occasions have produced rich fruit. If I do notice such areas, I will determine to give them both time and space in the future.

The Word

The word of God comes down to us through the Scriptures. May the Holy Spirit enlighten my mind and my heart to respond to the Gospel teachings.
(Please turn to the Scripture on the following pages. Inspiration points are there, should you need them. When you are ready, return here to continue.)

Conversation

What is stirring in me as I pray? Am I consoled, troubled, left cold? I imagine Jesus standing or sitting at my side, and I share my feelings with him.

Conclusion

Glory be to the Father, and to the Son and to the Holy Spirit,
As it was in the beginning, is now and ever shall be,
World without end. Amen.

Sunday 28 November
First Sunday of Advent

Luke 21:25–28.34–36

There will be signs in the sun, the moon, and the stars, and on the earth distress among nations confused by the roaring of the sea and the waves. People will faint from fear and foreboding of what is coming upon the world, for the powers of the heavens will be shaken. Then they will see 'the Son of Man coming in a cloud' with power and great glory. Now when these things begin to take place, stand up and raise your heads, because your redemption is drawing near.

Be on guard so that your hearts are not weighed down with dissipation and drunkenness and the worries of this life, and that day does not catch you unexpectedly, like a trap. For it will come upon all who live on the face of the whole earth. Be alert at all times, praying that you may have the strength to escape all these things that will take place, and to stand before the Son of Man.

- Advent is a season of hope and expectation. We are invited to prepare joyfully for the coming of Christ. He comes in history (his conception and birth), in mystery (through the sacraments, and especially the Eucharist) and in majesty (at the Last Day). In the first weeks of Advent the stress is on this third coming in majesty. Hence today's Gospel, which we have already prayed with in recent days. The old liturgical year has ended, and the new one has begun, with our calling to mind the Lord's final coming at the end of time. We look forward to it with happy anticipation, not with fear.

Monday 29 November

Matthew 8:5–11

When he entered Capernaum, a centurion came to him, appealing to him and saying, 'Lord, my servant is lying at home paralysed, in terrible distress.' And he said to him, 'I will come and cure him.' The centurion answered, 'Lord, I am not worthy to have you come under my roof; but only speak the word, and my servant will be healed. For I also am a man under authority, with soldiers under me; and I say to one, "Go", and he goes, and to another, "Come", and he comes, and to my slave, "Do this", and the slave does it.' When Jesus heard him, he was amazed and said to those who followed him, 'Truly I tell you, in no one in Israel have I found such faith. I tell you, many will come from east and west and will eat with Abraham and Isaac and Jacob in the kingdom of heaven.'

- Not many people could amaze Jesus, but this man does: he believes that Jesus can speak a word of healing, and that will be enough to cure his servant. Like the centurion, I may be used to giving and receiving instructions. Do I ever amaze Jesus with my faith?

- 'I will come and cure him.' Jesus reveals God's compassion and shows that the reign of God knows no boundaries. Not only Jews, but Gentiles from east and west, are welcomed by God into the kingdom. I pray to share God's breadth of vision.

Tuesday 30 November
Saint Andrew, Apostle

Matthew 4:18–22

As he walked by the Sea of Galilee, he saw two brothers, Simon, who is called Peter, and Andrew his brother, casting a net into the lake–for they were fishermen. And he said to them, 'Follow me, and I will make you fish for people.' Immediately they left their nets and followed him. As he went from there, he saw two other brothers, James son of Zebedee and his brother John, in the boat with their father Zebedee, mending their nets, and he called them. Immediately they left the boat and their father, and followed him.

- Andrew, together with his more famous brother Peter, is the first to be called by Jesus to follow him. This humble fisherman must have seen something very special in this man to make him immediately leave his nets, his livelihood, and follow him. What is Jesus' call to me in this period of my life? I pray for the grace not to be deaf to his call but prompt and generous in my response to it.
- Andrew was a member of that small yet amazing group of men who were ready to trust Jesus fully

and obey his incredible command to take the Gospel to all nations. It is thanks to Andrew and his companions that we, and hundreds of millions like us, believe in Jesus. I stand in awe and thanksgiving before this man and his Master.

Wednesday 1 December

Matthew 15:29–37

After Jesus had left that place, he passed along the Sea of Galilee, and he went up the mountain, where he sat down. Great crowds came to him, bringing with them the lame, the maimed, the blind, the mute, and many others. They put them at his feet, and he cured them, so that the crowd was amazed when they saw the mute speaking, the maimed whole, the lame walking, and the blind seeing. And they praised the God of Israel.

Then Jesus called his disciples to him and said, 'I have compassion for the crowd, because they have been with me now for three days and have nothing to eat; and I do not want to send them away hungry, for they might faint on the way.' The disciples said to him, 'Where are we to get enough bread in the desert to feed so great a crowd?' Jesus asked them, 'How many loaves have you?' They said, 'Seven, and a few small fish.' Then, ordering the crowd to sit down on the ground, he took the seven loaves and the fish; and after giving thanks he broke them and gave them to the disciples, and the disciples gave them to the crowds. And all of them ate and were filled; and they took up the broken pieces left over, seven baskets full.

- The people who came to Jesus were broken people. It was true then and is still true today. It is why I am here, listening to him. Where is my life broken? Where do I need his healing power? It is important to get in touch with that place in my life in order to get closer to him.

Thursday 2 December

Matthew 7:21. 24–27

'Not everyone who says to me, "Lord, Lord", will enter the kingdom of heaven, but only one who does the will of my Father in heaven.

'Everyone then who hears these words of mine and acts on them will be like a wise man who built his house on rock. The rain fell, the floods came, and the winds blew and beat on that house, but it did not fall, because it had been founded on rock. And everyone who hears these words of mine and does not act on them will be like a foolish man who built his house on sand. The rain fell, and the floods came, and the winds blew and beat against that house, and it fell– and great was its fall!'

- We all know that actions speak louder than words. We are told here that our eternal life depends upon our ability to act according to God's will. It is a stark message, but it is reassuring to know that our true efforts will reap their own rewards.

- I am challenged by Jesus to take time daily to reflect and discern the Father's will. Otherwise I will live a shallow existence that will not survive the floods and storms of life.

Friday 3 December

Matthew 9:27–31

As Jesus went on from there, two blind men followed him, crying loudly, 'Have mercy on us, Son of David!' When he entered the house, the blind men came to him; and Jesus said to them, 'Do you believe that I am able to do this?' They said to him, 'Yes, Lord.' Then he touched their eyes and said, 'According to your faith let it be done to you.' And their eyes were opened. Then Jesus sternly ordered them, 'See that no one knows of this.' But they went away and spread the news about him throughout that district.

- Desire is important. Knowing what I want–and having energy to pursue it–guides me. The Lord has desires for me, too. These desires can meet, as happened for the blind men. Their faith and need brought them to Jesus. I am invited to do the same, recognising that Jesus can transform my desires to bring them into harmony with his own.
- What are my deepest desires, and how influential are they in my living as a follower of Jesus? I pray to be in touch with Jesus' desire for me, knowing that my blindness can get in the way.

Saturday 4 December

Matthew 9:35–10:1.5a.6–8

Then Jesus went about all the cities and villages, teaching in their synagogues, and proclaiming the good news of the kingdom, and curing every disease and every sickness. When he saw the crowds, he had compassion for them, because they were harassed and helpless, like sheep without a shepherd. Then he said to his disciples, 'The harvest is plentiful, but the labourers are few; therefore ask the Lord of the harvest to send out labourers into his harvest.'

Then Jesus summoned his twelve disciples and gave them authority over unclean spirits, to cast them out, and to cure every disease and every sickness.

These twelve Jesus sent out with the following instructions: 'Go nowhere among the Gentiles, and enter no town of the Samaritans, but go rather to the lost sheep of the house of Israel. As you go, proclaim the good news, "The kingdom of heaven has come near." Cure the sick, raise the dead, cleanse the lepers, cast out demons. You received without payment; give without payment.'

- I travel in imagination with Jesus as he makes his journeys. I ask him what gives him so much energy to serve the sick, many of whom must have been frightening to look at and to touch. He talks with me about compassion, and I ask that my small heart grow to be as compassionate as his. I sense his compassion towards me and it comforts me.

- Jesus has a mission for me. Who are the 'lost sheep' today whom he may want me to help? Am I generous enough to do what he asks of me?

The Second Week of Advent

5–11 December 2021

Something to think and pray about each day this week:

Christmas can bring out the best in us to care for the needy. We are surrounded by charities looking for aid. We know that Jesus hears the cries of the poor, and he joins every carol singing group that tries to help.

Christmas also asks us to consider our honesty and integrity, for we know that many are poor, at home and abroad, because of the greed of others. Christmas is a reminder and a challenge that all can live with the dignity we have come to regard as a human right–with education, safety, shelter, food, water, employment, freedom. The Christ child, who was born poor, represents all the poor of the world, especially children. As he was born ordinary, he represents the God who meets, greets and helps us in the ordinary aspects of life.

The one who is to come is the one who will live and love according to these truths of human dignity and equality.

Donal Neary SJ,
Gospel Reflections for Sundays of Year C: Luke

The Presence of God

As I sit here, the beating of my heart,
the ebb and flow of my breathing, the movements of my mind
are all signs of God's ongoing creation of me.
I pause for a moment and become aware
of this presence of God within me.

Freedom

I will ask God's help
to be free from my own preoccupations,
to be open to God in this time of prayer,
to come to know, love and serve God more.

Consciousness

At this moment, Lord, I turn my thoughts to you.
I will leave aside my chores and preoccupations.
I will take rest and refreshment in your presence.

The Word

Now I turn to the Scripture set out for me this day. I read slowly over the words and see if any sentence or sentiment appeals to me.

(Please turn to the Scripture on the following pages. Inspiration points are there, should you need them. When you are ready, return here to continue.)

Conversation

Begin to talk to Jesus about the Scripture you have just read. What part of it strikes a chord in you? Perhaps the words of a friend–or some story you have heard recently–will slowly rise to the surface of your consciousness. If so, does the story throw light on what the Scripture passage may be saying to you?

Conclusion

Glory be to the Father, and to the Son and to the Holy Spirit,
As it was in the beginning, is now and ever shall be,
World without end. Amen.

Sunday 5 December
Second Sunday of Advent

Luke 3:1–6

In the fifteenth year of the reign of Emperor Tiberius, when Pontius Pilate was governor of Judea, and Herod was ruler of Galilee, and his brother Philip ruler of the region of Ituraea and Trachonitis, and Lysanias ruler of Abilene, during the high-priesthood of Annas and Caiaphas, the word of God came to John son of Zechariah in the wilderness. He went into all the region around the Jordan, proclaiming a baptism of repentance for the forgiveness of sins, as it is written in the book of the words of the prophet Isaiah,

'The voice of one crying out in the wilderness:
"Prepare the way of the Lord,
make his paths straight.
Every valley shall be filled,
and every mountain and hill shall be made low,
and the crooked shall be made straight,
and the rough ways made smooth;
and all flesh shall see the salvation of God."'

- Passage through the wilderness was an integral part of John's mission, as it was for Abraham, Moses, Elijah, and Jesus. Where, in all the hurly-burly of modern life, do we find a holy place where we can be apart and encounter God daily? Might it be here and now, on our desktop, laptop or mobile device, as we pray with Sacred Space?

- Do I believe that if I have the courage to place myself in the hands of my maker, I will feel the heavens open and grace rain down upon me, transforming my desert, making the crooked straight, the rough places smooth, until–at last–I will see the salvation of God?

Monday 6 December

Luke 5:17–26

One day, while he was teaching, Pharisees and teachers of the law were sitting nearby (they had come from every village of Galilee and Judea and from Jerusalem); and the power of the Lord was with him to heal. Just then some men came, carrying a paralysed man on a bed. They were trying to bring him in and lay him before Jesus; but finding no way to bring him in because of the crowd, they went up on the roof and let him down with his bed through the tiles into the middle of the crowd in front of Jesus. When he saw their faith, he said, 'Friend, your sins are forgiven you.' Then the scribes and the Pharisees began to question, 'Who is this who is speaking blasphemies? Who can forgive sins but God alone?' When Jesus perceived their questionings, he answered them, 'Why do you raise such questions in your hearts? Which is easier, to say, "Your sins are forgiven you", or to say, "Stand up and walk"? But so that you may know that the Son of Man has authority on earth to forgive sins'–he said to the one who was paralysed–'I say to you, stand up and take your bed and go to your home.' Immediately he stood up before them, took what he had been lying on, and went to his home, glorifying God. Amazement seized all of them, and they glorified God and were filled with awe, saying, 'We have seen strange things today.'

- Sometimes, we need help from others to ask for healing, or to help others do so. It was the faith of his friends and not the paralysed man's own faith to which Jesus responded, 'And when Jesus saw their faith, he said to the paralytic, "My friend, your sins are forgiven."' When we forgive, and when we are forgiven, a crippling burden is lifted from our shoulders. We can then, like the man in this episode, rise and walk.

Tuesday 7 December

Matthew 18:12–14

What do you think? If a shepherd has a hundred sheep, and one of them has gone astray, does he not leave the ninety-nine on the mountains and go in search of the one that went astray? And if he finds it, truly I tell you, he rejoices over it more than over the ninety-nine that never went astray. So it is not the will of your Father in heaven that one of these little ones should be lost.

- Let us never grow accustomed to this parable. It is the most astonishing suggestion you could imagine. Modern business would focus on the ninety-nine well-behaved and conformist sheep. Jesus turns our eyes to that bit of ourselves that wants to do our own thing, go our own way, even when it is self-destructive. As parents have learned with heartbreak, it is only love that will save the lost sheep.

- I cling to that last assurance: 'It is not the will of your Father that one of these little ones should be lost.'

Wednesday 8 December
The Immaculate Conception of the Blessed Virgin Mary

Luke 1:26–38

In the sixth month the angel Gabriel was sent by God to a town in Galilee called Nazareth, to a virgin engaged to a man whose name was Joseph, of the house of David. The virgin's name was Mary. And he came to her and said, 'Greetings, favoured one! The Lord is with you.' But she was much perplexed by his words and pondered what sort of greeting this might be. The angel said to her, 'Do not be afraid, Mary, for you have found favour with God. And now, you will conceive in your womb and bear a son, and you will name him Jesus. He will be great, and will be called the Son of the Most High, and the Lord God will give to him the throne of his ancestor David. He will reign over the house of Jacob for ever, and of his kingdom there will be no end.' Mary said to the angel, 'How can this be, since I am a virgin?' The angel said to her, 'The Holy Spirit will come upon you, and the power of the Most High will overshadow you; therefore the child to be born will be holy; he will be called Son of God. And now, your relative Elizabeth in her old age has also conceived a son; and this is the sixth month for her who was said to be barren. For nothing will be impossible with God.' Then Mary said, 'Here am I, the servant of the Lord; let it be with me according to your word.' Then the angel departed from her.

- Repeating a phrase in prayer may make it go deep within us. It's like a favourite piece of music that we can hum over and over again. It is part of us. 'I am the servant of the Lord' was such a phrase for Mary, spoken first at one of the biggest moments in her life. In dry times of prayer, a sentence like that can occupy mind and heart and raise us close to God.

Thursday 9 December

Matthew 11:11–15

Truly I tell you, among those born of women no one has arisen greater than John the Baptist; yet the least in the kingdom of heaven is greater than he. From the days of John the Baptist until now the kingdom of heaven has suffered violence, and the violent take it by force. For all the prophets and the law prophesied until John came; and if you are willing to accept it, he is Elijah who is to come. Let anyone with ears listen!

- God does not force himself upon us. We must ourselves seize the kingdom. In his book, *Heaven*

Taken by Storm, seventeenth-century Puritan pastor Thomas Watson asks: 'Do we use violence in prayer? Is the wind of the Spirit filling our sails? Do we pray in the morning as if we were to die at night? Do we thirst for the living God? Is our desire constant? Is this spiritual pulse always beating?'

- 'Let anyone with ears listen!' What is Jesus saying to me in this time of meditation?

Friday 10 December

Matthew 11:16–19

'But to what will I compare this generation? It is like children sitting in the market-places and calling to one another,

"We played the flute for you, and you did not dance;
we wailed, and you did not mourn."

For John came neither eating nor drinking, and they say, "He has a demon"; the Son of Man came eating and drinking, and they say, "Look, a glutton and a drunkard, a friend of tax-collectors and sinners!" Yet wisdom is vindicated by her deeds.'

- Jesus notices those who sit back and do nothing except judge others. John is too strange, while Jesus is too normal for such people. Am I occasionally cynical and critical? Do I disparage the humble efforts of others when they do their best?
- Do I bear faithful witness to Jesus by good deeds? Such deeds may be costly, but the ultimate course of events will reveal that they were wise decisions.

Saturday 11 December

Matthew 17:9a.10–13

As they were coming down the mountain, Jesus ordered them, 'Tell no one about the vision until after the Son of Man has been raised from the dead.' And the disciples asked him, 'Why, then, do the scribes say that Elijah must come first?' He replied, 'Elijah is indeed coming and will restore all things; but I tell you that Elijah has already come, and they did not recognise him, but they did to him whatever they pleased. So also the Son of Man is about to suffer at their hands.' Then the disciples understood that he was speaking to them about John the Baptist.

- Shortly before this scene, Jesus' disciples saw Jesus transfigured in glory and flanked by Moses and Elijah, so obviously the latter was still on their minds. They ask Jesus for confirmation regarding the role of Elijah as forerunner of the End Time.
- Jesus' reply was unexpected in more ways than one: the real forerunner is John the Baptist, he has been badly treated, and this will also be the fate of Jesus himself.
- By our prayer this Christmas, we can ensure that the newly born Jesus is welcome in our lives, even if his message turns some of our values on their heads.

The Third Week of Advent
12–18 December 2021

Something to think and pray about each day this week:

She got off at the same stop as me. The busyness of the bus was drowned out by her cry: 'My bags ... they're gone!' Someone had taken her last-minute shopping. Presents from Santa, gifts for under the Christmas tree, kindly items for neighbours, clothes for the day and the necessary ingredients to enhance the dinner–all gone. What upset her most was trying to think of what she was going to say to some of the people she'd bought gifts for, especially her children. She could see their disappointed faces and was stumped as how she could explain what had happened. Christmas Eve–the season of good will–drained away before her eyes.

The world can challenge our efforts at good will. At times it might appear to us that trying to make the world a better place is akin to pushing a rock up a steep hill, but the Christian cannot give in to despair. The God we believe in would never have joined us on our dusty roads if he didn't believe in the triumph of the good. If despair was king, hope would never have been born among us in human flesh.

Alan Hilliard, *Dipping into Advent*

The Presence of God

At any time of the day or night we can call on Jesus. He is always waiting, listening for our call. What a wonderful blessing.

No phone needed, no e-mails, just a whisper.

Freedom

If God were trying to tell me something, would I know?

If God were reassuring me or challenging me, would I notice?

I ask for the grace to be free of my own preoccupations and open to what God may be saying to me.

Consciousness

Help me, Lord, become more conscious of your presence. Teach me to recognise your presence in others. Fill my heart with gratitude for the times your love has been shown to me through the care of others.

The Word

In this expectant state of mind, please turn to the text for the day with confidence. Believe that the Holy Spirit is present and may reveal whatever the passage has to say to you. Read reflectively, listening with a third ear to what may be going on in your heart.

(Please turn to the Scripture on the following pages. Inspiration points are there, should you need them. When you are ready, return here to continue.)

Conversation

As I talk to Jesus, may I also learn to pause and listen.
I picture the gentleness in his eyes and the love in his smile.
I can be totally honest with Jesus as I tell him my worries and cares.
I will open my heart to Jesus as I tell him my fears and doubts.
I will ask him to help me place myself fully in his care, knowing that he always desires good for me.

Conclusion

I thank God for these moments we have spent together and for any insights I have been given concerning the text.

Sunday 12 December
Third Sunday of Advent

Luke 3:10–18

And the crowds asked him, 'What then should we do?' In reply he said to them, 'Whoever has two coats must share with anyone who has none; and whoever has food must do likewise.' Even tax-collectors came to be baptised, and they asked him, 'Teacher, what should we do?' He said to them, 'Collect no more than the amount prescribed for you.' Soldiers also asked him, 'And we, what should we do?' He said to them, 'Do not extort money from anyone by threats or false accusation, and be satisfied with your wages.'

As the people were filled with expectation, and all were questioning in their hearts concerning John, whether he might be the Messiah, John answered all of them by saying, 'I baptise you with water; but one who is more powerful than I is coming; I am not worthy to untie the thong of his sandals. He will baptise you with the Holy Spirit and fire. His winnowing-fork is in his hand, to clear his threshing-floor and to gather the wheat into his granary; but the chaff he will burn with unquenchable fire.'

So, with many other exhortations, he proclaimed the good news to the people.

- John doesn't ask tax-collectors to stop collecting or tell soldiers to desert. His message is simple: social justice. Share what you have, be honest, do not oppress people. He does not call for heroics. But sometimes heroics seem easier than living daily life well. How can I bring the divine into my ordinary actions and make my faith a living thing?

- What must I do to prepare to meet the Messiah?

Monday 13 December

Matthew 21:23–27

When he entered the temple, the chief priests and the elders of the people came to him as he was teaching, and said, 'By what authority are you doing these things, and who gave you this authority?' Jesus said to them, 'I will also ask you one question; if you tell me the answer, then I will also tell you by what authority I do these things. Did the baptism of John come from heaven, or was it of human origin?' And they argued with one another, 'If we say, "From heaven", he will say to us, "Why then did you not believe him?" But if we say, "Of human origin", we are afraid of the crowd; for all regard John as a prophet.' So they answered Jesus, 'We do not know.' And he said to them, 'Neither will I tell you by what authority I am doing these things.'

- What authority does Jesus have? If he turned up today, would we want to see his qualifications before allowing him to preach? Or would his attitudes, words and deeds resonate deeply within us, so that we would say, 'All that he says and does, and the way he does it, are just right'?

- God's wisdom is not confined to the worldly wise. God's grace is not confined to those of whom the world approves. I consider how I might be open to revelation from unusual sources, unlikely people and in unexpected places.

Tuesday 14 December

Matthew 21:28–32

'What do you think? A man had two sons; he went to the first and said, "Son, go and work in the vineyard today." He answered, "I will not"; but later he changed his mind and went. The father went to the second and said the same; and he answered, "I go, sir"; but he did not go. Which of the two did the will of his father?' They said, 'The first.' Jesus said to them, 'Truly I tell you, the tax-collectors and the prostitutes are going into the kingdom of God ahead of you. For John came to you in the way of righteousness and you did not believe him, but the tax-collectors and the prostitutes believed him; and even after you saw it, you did not change your minds and believe him.

- In this parable, the tax collectors and prostitutes–those most despised and rejected by society–are ahead of the self-righteous ones. They were the ones who were open to the word of God and to change.

- Lord, you continually invite me to fullness of life. I pray that through Sacred Space my faith in you may grow ever deeper and that it may be expressed by my desire to serve others.

Wednesday 15 December

Luke 7:18b–23

The disciples of John reported all these things to him. So John summoned two of his disciples and sent them to the Lord to ask, 'Are you the one who is to come, or are we to wait for another?' When the men had come to him, they said, 'John the Baptist has sent us to you to ask, "Are you the one who is to come, or are we to wait for another?"' Jesus had just then cured many people of diseases, plagues, and evil spirits, and had given sight to many who were blind. And he answered them, 'Go and tell John what you have seen and heard: the blind receive their sight, the lame walk, the lepers are cleansed, the deaf hear, the dead are raised, the poor have good news brought to them. And blessed is anyone who takes no offence at me.'

- The readings before Christmas search my heart profoundly. Am I longing for Jesus to come more deeply into my life this Advent? Or am I waiting for God to come in some other form? Would I prefer a different kind of 'good news' than the Gospel about Jesus?

- The Jews wanted a political Messiah who would dramatically terminate their oppression by the Romans. But Jesus has good news primarily for the blind, the lame, the lepers, the deaf, the dead and the poor. I ask him that I may not get lost in political issues but share my love with those who are marginalised and unwanted by the world.

Thursday 16 December

Luke 7:24–30

When John's messengers had gone, Jesus began to speak to the crowds about John: 'What did you go out into the wilderness to look at? A reed shaken by the wind? What then did you go out to see? Someone dressed in soft robes? Look, those who put on fine clothing and live in luxury are in royal palaces. What then did you go out to see? A prophet? Yes, I tell you, and more than a prophet. This is the one about whom it is written,

> "See, I am sending my messenger ahead of you,
> who will prepare your way before you."

I tell you, among those born of women no one is greater than John; yet the least in the kingdom of God is greater than he.' (And all the people who heard this, including the tax-collectors, acknowledged the justice of God, because they had been baptised with John's baptism. But by refusing to be baptised by him, the

Pharisees and the lawyers rejected God's purpose for themselves.)

- What do I go out to see? What are my true values? What impresses me? Jesus was impressed by John because he expressed God's values and chose simplicity of life. I ask him if he is impressed by me, and I listen in my heart to what he says to me.

Friday 17 December

Matthew 1:1–17

An account of the genealogy of Jesus the Messiah, the son of David, the son of Abraham.

Abraham was the father of Isaac, and Isaac the father of Jacob, and Jacob the father of Judah and his brothers, and Judah the father of Perez and Zerah by Tamar, and Perez the father of Hezron, and Hezron the father of Aram, and Aram the father of Aminadab, and Aminadab the father of Nahshon, and Nahshon the father of Salmon, and Salmon the father of Boaz by Rahab, and Boaz the father of Obed by Ruth, and Obed the father of Jesse, and Jesse the father of King David.

And David was the father of Solomon by the wife of Uriah, and Solomon the father of Rehoboam, and Rehoboam the father of Abijah, and Abijah the father of Asaph, and Asaph the father of Jehoshaphat, and Jehoshaphat the father of Joram, and Joram the father of Uzziah, and Uzziah the father of Jotham, and Jotham the father of Ahaz, and Ahaz the father of Hezekiah, and Hezekiah the father of Manasseh, and Manasseh the father of Amos, and Amos the father of Josiah, and Josiah the father of Jechoniah and his brothers, at the time of the deportation to Babylon.

And after the deportation to Babylon: Jechoniah was the father of Salathiel, and Salathiel the father of Zerubbabel, and Zerubbabel the father of Abiud, and Abiud the father of Eliakim, and Eliakim the father of Azor, and Azor the father of Zadok, and Zadok the father of Achim, and Achim the father of Eliud, and Eliud the father of Eleazar, and Eleazar the father of Matthan, and Matthan the father of Jacob, and Jacob the father of Joseph the husband of Mary, of whom Jesus was born, who is called the Messiah.

So all the generations from Abraham to David are fourteen generations; and from David to the deportation to Babylon, fourteen generations; and from the deportation to Babylon to the Messiah, fourteen generations.

- This Gospel weaves the threads of the long history that eventually brings us to Jesus. His family tree is a mix of holy and unholy figures, public sinners and outcasts. Yet each played an important role and no one's life was insignificant in God's plan. Jesus does own his family story. He does not airbrush out any of his ancestors. Do I?

- Lord, I thank you for all who have been carriers of your grace to me. Let not my limitations and inadequacy impede me from believing that I am important. Let me play my part in being a carrier of your love to the world.

Saturday 18 December

Matthew 1:18–25

Now the birth of Jesus the Messiah took place in this way. When his mother Mary had been engaged to Joseph, but before they lived together, she was found to be with child from the Holy Spirit. Her husband Joseph, being a righteous man and unwilling to expose her to public disgrace, planned to dismiss her quietly. But just when he had resolved to do this, an angel of the Lord appeared to him in a dream and said, 'Joseph, son of David, do not be afraid to take Mary as your wife, for the child conceived in her is from the Holy Spirit. She will bear a son, and you are to name him Jesus, for he will save his people from their sins.' All this took place to fulfil what had been spoken by the Lord through the prophet:

> 'Look, the virgin shall conceive and bear a son,
> and they shall name him Emmanuel',

which means, 'God is with us.' When Joseph awoke from sleep, he did as the angel of the Lord commanded him; he took her as his wife, but had no marital relations with her until she had borne a son; and he named him Jesus.

- In a mysterious, miraculous way, known only in faith, the Spirit's action brings the gift to the world of the God-person, the human in the divine and the divine in the human in a totally physical and spiritual way. In the humanity of Mary, Jesus is growing from embryo to child. In the faith of Joseph, the call first came to all of us to believe the mystery. In prayer we might picture Mary and Joseph talking together about all that has happened and picture the Holy Spirit, in the love and in the atmosphere around them. Bring that presence of the Spirit into your day today.

The Fourth Week of Advent/Christmas

19–25 December 2021

Something to think and pray about each day this week:

God has visited his people in and through the person of his Son, Jesus. This visitation reveals the tender mercy of God. Jesus' coming is spoken of as the rising Sun from on high, bringing light to those who live in darkness and in the shadow of death. The sun is the source of light and life. In an even more fundamental sense, Jesus is the source of light and life. In revealing God's tender mercy, Jesus brings the light of God's merciful love into the darkness of our lives, and he also offers us a sharing in God's own life, thereby scattering the shadow that death casts over us. The true meaning of Christmas is to be found here. In celebrating the birth of Jesus, we are celebrating the coming of God's light and life, a light that no darkness can overcome and a life that is stronger than all forms of death. Christmas is the feast of Jesus, the light of life. It is a truly hopeful feast because it proclaims that we need no longer remain in darkness or in the shadow of death.

Martin Hogan, *The Word of God Is Living and Active*

The Presence of God

Dear Jesus, as I call on you today, I realise that often I come asking for favours. Today I'd like just to be in your presence.

Freedom

It is so easy to get caught up with the trappings of wealth in this life.
Grant, O Lord, that I may be free from greed and selfishness.
Remind me that the best things in life are free:
Love, laughter, caring and sharing.

Consciousness

How am I really feeling? Lighthearted? Heavyhearted?
I may be very much at peace, happy to be here.
Equally, I may be frustrated, worried or angry.
I acknowledge how I really am. It is the real me whom the Lord loves.

The Word

Lord Jesus, you became human to communicate with me.
You walked and worked on this earth.
You endured the heat and struggled with the cold.
All your time on this earth was spent in caring for humanity.
You healed the sick, you raised the dead.
Most important of all, you saved me from death.

(Please turn to the Scripture on the following pages. Inspiration points are there, should you need them. When you are ready, return here to continue.)

Conversation

Do I notice myself reacting as I pray with the word of God? Do I feel challenged, comforted, angry? Imagining Jesus sitting or standing by me, I speak out my feelings, as one trusted friend to another.

Conclusion

Glory be to the Father, and to the Son, and to the Holy Spirit,
As it was in the beginning, is now and ever shall be,
World without end. Amen.

Sunday 19 December
Fourth Sunday of Advent

Luke 1:39–45

In those days Mary set out and went with haste to a Judean town in the hill country, where she entered the house of Zechariah and greeted Elizabeth. When Elizabeth heard Mary's greeting, the child leapt in her womb. And Elizabeth was filled with the Holy Spirit and exclaimed with a loud cry, 'Blessed are you among women, and blessed is the fruit of your womb. And why has this happened to me, that the mother of my Lord comes to me? For as soon as I heard the sound of your greeting, the child in my womb leapt for joy. And blessed is she who believed that there would be a fulfilment of what was spoken to her by the Lord.'

- Lord, as Christmas draws ever closer, free me from being self-absorbed and self-centred. Instead fill me with eagerness and generosity of heart. Like Mary, may I too go out in loving service of others and experience your Love leaping up in me and in those with whom I come in contact.

Monday 20 December

Luke 1:26–38

In the sixth month the angel Gabriel was sent by God to a town in Galilee called Nazareth, to a virgin engaged to a man whose name was Joseph, of the house of David. The virgin's name was Mary. And he came to her and said, 'Greetings, favoured one! The Lord is with you.' But she was much perplexed by his words and pondered what sort of greeting this might be. The angel said to her, 'Do not be afraid, Mary, for you have found favour with God. And now, you will conceive in your womb and bear a son, and you will name him Jesus. He will be great, and will be called the Son of the Most High, and the Lord God will give to him the throne of his ancestor David. He will reign over the house of Jacob for ever, and of his kingdom there will be no end.' Mary said to the angel, 'How can this be, since I am a virgin?' The angel said to her, 'The Holy Spirit will come upon you, and the power of the Most High will overshadow you; therefore the child to be born will be holy; he will be called Son of God. And now, your relative Elizabeth in her old age has also conceived a son; and this is the sixth month for her who was said to be barren. For nothing will be impossible with God.' Then Mary said, 'Here am I, the servant of the Lord; let it be with me according to your word.' Then the angel departed from her.

- In our lives there are turning points whereby we may experience an invitation to embrace something difficult rather than discard it; something that wrecks our dreams for ourselves or for our loved ones. There's a need to discern the spirits.

- If something is disconcerting, that doesn't mean that it's bad. How would your better self respond?

Tuesday 21 December

Luke 1:39–45

In those days Mary set out and went with haste to a Judean town in the hill country, where she entered the house of Zechariah and greeted Elizabeth. When Elizabeth heard Mary's greeting, the child leapt in her womb. And Elizabeth was filled with the Holy Spirit and exclaimed with a loud cry, 'Blessed are you among women, and blessed is the fruit of your womb. And why has this happened to me, that the mother of my Lord comes to me? For as soon as I heard the sound of your greeting, the child in my womb leapt for joy. And blessed is she who believed that there would be a fulfilment of what was spoken to her by the Lord.'

- The journey from Nazareth to Ein Karim was long and uncomfortable for Mary, who carries the secret–she is the womb of God. This visitation was a Eucharistic moment. The light of Christ comes to Elizabeth through Mary. Both women rejoice! Mary's one desire is to go out in loving service to help her pregnant cousin.

Wednesday 22 December

Luke 1:46–56

And Mary said,
'My soul magnifies the Lord,
and my spirit rejoices in God my Saviour,
for he has looked with favour on the lowliness of
his servant.
Surely, from now on all generations will call me
blessed;
for the Mighty One has done great things for me,
and holy is his name.
His mercy is for those who fear him
from generation to generation.
He has shown strength with his arm;
he has scattered the proud in the thoughts of
their hearts.
He has brought down the powerful from their
thrones,
and lifted up the lowly;
he has filled the hungry with good things,
and sent the rich away empty.
He has helped his servant Israel,
in remembrance of his mercy,
according to the promise he made to our ancestors,
to Abraham and to his descendants for ever.'
And Mary remained with her for about three
months and then returned to her home.

- I imagine that I am invited to stay with Elizabeth and Mary for the three months they spend together. I observe what they say and do and how quietly happy they both are as they carry the mystery of God in their wombs.
- Mary praises the God who turns human history upside down. God scatters the proud, pulls down the mighty and dismisses the rich. In their place he exalts the unimportant ones and feeds the starving. Do I value the despised and downtrodden of this world above the famous and the wealthy? I talk to Mary about this.

Thursday 23 December

Luke 1:57–66

Now the time came for Elizabeth to give birth, and she bore a son. Her neighbours and relatives heard that the Lord had shown his great mercy to her, and they rejoiced with her.

On the eighth day they came to circumcise the child, and they were going to name him Zechariah after his father. But his mother said, 'No; he is to be called John.' They said to her, 'None of your relatives has this name.' Then they began motioning to his father to find out what name he wanted to give him. He asked for a writing-tablet and wrote, 'His name is John.' And all of them were amazed. Immediately his mouth was opened and his tongue freed, and he began to speak, praising God. Fear came over all their neighbours, and all these things were talked about throughout the entire hill country of Judea. All who heard them pondered them and said, 'What then will this child become?' For, indeed, the hand of the Lord was with him.

- I join in the excitement around the birth of Elizabeth's baby. I become aware that God is fulfilling his plans through human beings who collaborate. God wants the child to be called John, and this is what happens. In Luke's understanding of salvation, what God decides will eventually be fulfilled. I ask for faith to believe this and to be free of anxiety.

Friday 24 December

Luke 1:67–79

Then his father Zechariah was filled with the Holy Spirit and spoke this prophecy:

'Blessed be the Lord God of Israel,
for he has looked favourably on his people and
redeemed them.
He has raised up a mighty saviour for us
in the house of his servant David,
as he spoke through the mouth of his holy
prophets from of old,

that we would be saved from our enemies and
from the hand of all who hate us.
Thus he has shown the mercy promised to our
ancestors,
and has remembered his holy covenant,
the oath that he swore to our ancestor Abraham,
to grant us that we, being rescued from the hands
of our enemies,
might serve him without fear, in holiness and
righteousness
before him all our days.
And you, child, will be called the prophet of the
Most High;
for you will go before the Lord to prepare his ways,
to give knowledge of salvation to his people
by the forgiveness of their sins.
By the tender mercy of our God,
the dawn from on high will break upon us,
to give light to those who sit in darkness and in
the shadow of death,
to guide our feet into the way of peace.'

- The Benedictus is a prayer of prophecy about the coming of the Saviour. This 'Most High' that Zechariah mentions comes not in a cloud of glory but as a vulnerable child, with an ordinary family, in a cold stable. That is the kind of God we have.

Saturday 25 December
The Nativity of the Lord

John 1:1–18

In the beginning was the Word, and the Word was with God, and the Word was God. He was in the beginning with God. All things came into being through him, and without him not one thing came into being. What has come into being in him was life, and the life was the light of all people. The light shines in the darkness, and the darkness did not overcome it.

There was a man sent from God, whose name was John. He came as a witness to testify to the light, so that all might believe through him. He himself was not the light, but he came to testify to the light. The true light, which enlightens everyone, was coming into the world.

He was in the world, and the world came into being through him; yet the world did not know him. He came to what was his own, and his own people did not accept him. But to all who received him, who believed in his name, he gave power to become children of God, who were born, not of blood or of the will of the flesh or of the will of man, but of God.

And the Word became flesh and lived among us, and we have seen his glory, the glory as of a father's only son, full of grace and truth. (John testified to him and cried out, 'This was he of whom I said, "He who comes after me ranks ahead of me because he was before me.'") From his fullness we have all received, grace upon grace. The law indeed was given through Moses; grace and truth came through Jesus Christ. No one has ever seen God. It is God the only Son, who is close to the Father's heart, who has made him known.

- It has been an eventful year that leaves lasting memories. We have the fidelity of God to sustain us in the many challenges of life. We need light in the darkness and hope in the uncertainty that is around us. God has given us the Eternal Word and the living word of scripture to guide us. We pray to welcome and appreciate those words more fully, asking that our words be in harmony with them. What word does the Lord desire me to take with me as I enter the New Year?

First Week of Christmas

26 December 2021–1 January 2022

Something to think and pray about each day this week:

Faith, prayer, Mass and the Church can bring us through a lot in bad days.

Prayer can be a valued part of family life. In all the different stresses today of family life, if we teach by word and example the value and place of prayer in their lives we have given a lot. The example of love and care, even in stressful times, can never be underestimated.

Some pray at night or in the morning, before a meal or leaving the house; Mass and the inclusion of prayer at high points of family life are ways of including prayer in family life. Family is the school of faith and the place of God in the everyday world.

Donal Neary SJ,
Gospel Reflections for Sundays of Year C: Luke

The Presence of God

Dear Jesus, I come to you today longing for your presence. I desire to love you as you love me. May nothing ever separate me from you.

Freedom

Lord, grant me the grace to have freedom of the Spirit. Cleanse my heart and soul so that I may live joyously in your love.

Consciousness

Where am I with God? With others?
Do I have something to be grateful for? Then I give thanks.
Is there something I am sorry for? Then I ask forgiveness.

The Word

The word of God comes down to us through the Scriptures. May the Holy Spirit enlighten my mind and my heart to respond to the Gospel teachings.
(Please turn to the Scripture on the following pages. Inspiration points are there, should you need them. When you are ready, return here to continue.)

Conversation

How has God's word moved me? Has it left me cold?
Has it consoled me or moved me to act in a new way?
I imagine Jesus standing or sitting beside me;
I turn and share my feelings with him.

Conclusion

I thank God for these moments we have spent together and for any insights I have been given concerning the text.

Sunday 26 December
The Holy Family of Jesus, Mary and Joseph

Luke 2:41–52

Now every year his parents went to Jerusalem for the festival of the Passover. And when he was twelve years old, they went up as usual for the festival. When the festival was ended and they started to return, the boy Jesus stayed behind in Jerusalem, but his parents did not know it. Assuming that he was in the group of travellers, they went a day's journey. Then they started to look for him among their relatives and friends. When they did not find him, they returned to Jerusalem to search for him. After three days they found him in the temple, sitting among the teachers, listening to them and asking them questions. And all who heard him were amazed at his understanding and his answers. When his parents saw him they were astonished; and his mother said to him, 'Child, why have you treated us like this? Look, your father and I have been searching for you in great anxiety.' He said to them, 'Why were you searching for me? Did you not know that I must be in my Father's house?' But they did not understand what he said to them. Then he went down with them and came to Nazareth, and was obedient to them. His mother treasured all these things in her heart.

And Jesus increased in wisdom and in years, and in divine and human favour.

- Lord, you have tasted human uncertainties and the difficulties of survival. Your mother, so blissfully happy when she prayed the Magnificat, had to adjust rapidly to homelessness and the life of an asylum-seeker. Let me be equally unsurprisable when plans go awry and you ask me to taste uncertainties.

Monday 27 December
Saint John, Apostle

John 20:1a. 2–8

Early on the first day of the week, while it was still dark, Mary Magdalene came to the tomb and saw that the stone had been removed from the tomb. So she ran and went to Simon Peter and the other disciple, the one whom Jesus loved, and said to them, 'They have taken the Lord out of the tomb, and we do not know where they have laid him.' Then Peter and the other disciple set out and went towards the tomb. The two were running together, but the other disciple outran Peter and reached the tomb first. He bent down to look in and saw the linen wrappings lying there, but he did not go in. Then Simon Peter came, following him, and went into the tomb. He saw the linen wrappings lying there, and the cloth that had been on Jesus' head, not lying with the linen wrappings but rolled up in a place by itself. Then the other disciple, who reached the tomb first, also went in, and he saw and believed.

- It is sometimes tempting to cling to the glow of Christmas. While I value the gift of this season, this Easter scene reminds me that faith calls me to move on, to seek the Risen Lord.
- When Mary Magdalene did not find Jesus where she expected, she went first to her community. As questions arise for me, I bring them to God and to others whom I trust.

Tuesday 28 December

Matthew 2:13–18

Now after they had left, an angel of the Lord appeared to Joseph in a dream and said, 'Get up, take the child and his mother, and flee to Egypt, and remain there until I tell you; for Herod is about to search for the child, to destroy him.' Then Joseph got up, took the child and his mother by night, and went to Egypt, and remained there until the death of Herod. This was to fulfil what had been spoken by the Lord through the prophet, 'Out of Egypt I have called my son.'

When Herod saw that he had been tricked by the wise men, he was infuriated, and he sent and killed all the children in and around Bethlehem who were two years old or under, according to the time that he had learned from the wise men. Then was fulfilled what had been spoken through the prophet Jeremiah:

'A voice was heard in Ramah,
wailing and loud lamentation,

Rachel weeping for her children;
she refused to be consoled, because they are no
more.'

- Starting with the scene of the Holy Family forced to flee into Egypt, we reflect in our prayer on the whole Jewish people finding themselves in captivity in Egypt (and on their eventual release being withheld by Pharaoh, until first the blood of a child flowed in every house of his own population).
- The road to the fullness of freedom for the Jewish people in the Promised Land had tragic turns. The same was true of the road Jesus himself walked, and the same is true, one way or another, of the road each of us walks.

Wednesday 29 December

Luke 2:22–35

When the time came for their purification according to the law of Moses, they brought him up to Jerusalem to present him to the Lord (as it is written in the law of the Lord, 'Every firstborn male shall be designated as holy to the Lord'), and they offered a sacrifice according to what is stated in the law of the Lord, 'a pair of turtle-doves or two young pigeons.'

Now there was a man in Jerusalem whose name was Simeon; this man was righteous and devout, looking forward to the consolation of Israel, and the

Holy Spirit rested on him. It had been revealed to him by the Holy Spirit that he would not see death before he had seen the Lord's Messiah. Guided by the Spirit, Simeon came into the temple; and when the parents brought in the child Jesus, to do for him what was customary under the law, Simeon took him in his arms and praised God, saying,

> 'Master, now you are dismissing your servant in
> peace,
> according to your word;
> for my eyes have seen your salvation,
> which you have prepared in the presence of all
> peoples,
> a light for revelation to the Gentiles
> and for glory to your people Israel.'

And the child's father and mother were amazed at what was being said about him. Then Simeon blessed them and said to his mother Mary, 'This child is destined for the falling and the rising of many in Israel, and to be a sign that will be opposed so that the inner thoughts of many will be revealed–and a sword will pierce your own soul too.'

- Lord, in Simeon I see hope triumphant, hope richly rewarded. The years of waiting–the centuries before he himself was born and the long years that he had lived–did not blunt the edge of his faith. His hope and yearning left him alive to the prompting of God, ready to hear it when it came. Grant that I may learn from him.

Thursday 30 December

Luke 2:36–40

There was also a prophet, Anna the daughter of Phanuel, of the tribe of Asher. She was of a great age, having lived with her husband for seven years after her marriage, then as a widow to the age of eighty-four. She never left the temple but worshipped there with fasting and prayer night and day. At that moment she came, and began to praise God and to speak about the child to all who were looking for the redemption of Jerusalem.

When they had finished everything required by the law of the Lord, they returned to Galilee, to their own town of Nazareth. The child grew and became strong, filled with wisdom; and the favour of God was upon him.

- The life of Anna was hidden away in the temple. The life of Jesus as he grew from childhood to manhood was hidden for thirty years in an obscure village. In this hidden time, Jesus grows. He becomes strong, filled with wisdom and God's favour.
- Lord, let me value the hidden quality of prayer. Let me never doubt the value of 'wasting time' hidden with you before the Father.

Friday 31 December

John 1:1–18

In the beginning was the Word, and the Word was with God, and the Word was God. He was in the beginning with God. All things came into being through him, and without him not one thing came into being. What has come into being in him was life, and the life was the light of all people. The light shines in the darkness, and the darkness did not overcome it.

There was a man sent from God, whose name was John. He came as a witness to testify to the light, so that all might believe through him. He himself was not the light, but he came to testify to the light. The true light, which enlightens everyone, was coming into the world.

He was in the world, and the world came into being through him; yet the world did not know him. He came to what was his own, and his own people did not accept him. But to all who received him, who believed in his name, he gave power to become children of God, who were born, not of blood or of the will of the flesh or of the will of man, but of God.

And the Word became flesh and lived among us, and we have seen his glory, the glory as of a father's only son, full of grace and truth. (John testified to him and cried out, 'This was he of whom I said, "He who comes after me ranks ahead of me because he was before me."') From his fullness we have all received, grace upon grace. The law indeed was given through Moses; grace and truth came through Jesus Christ. No one has ever seen God. It is God the only Son, who is close to the Father's heart, who has made him known.

- We come to the end of a year and listen to what God's word says to us. It helps us look back to learn and look forward in hope. God's word is a creative Word who gives life to all, in love.

Saturday 1 January
Mary, the Mother of God

Luke 2:16–21

So they went with haste and found Mary and Joseph, and the child lying in the manger. When they saw this, they made known what had been told them about this child; and all who heard it were amazed at what the shepherds told them. But Mary treasured all these words and pondered them in her heart. The shepherds returned, glorifying and praising God for all they had heard and seen, as it had been told them.

After eight days had passed, it was time to circumcise the child; and he was called Jesus, the name given by the angel before he was conceived in the womb.

- As we begin this new year we find an amazing piece of Good News waiting to cheer our hearts! God has become human and is no longer remote or shadowy. We all feel comfortable with a baby, and when it smiles at us, our tired hearts are filled with joy. We can get in on the scene by knocking at the door and are greeted by Mary's smile. Take time to sit with the little family and the shepherds, in silent wonder. Perhaps you forgot to bring a gift, but it doesn't matter: you've brought yourself!

- Whenever you see a baby this year, make the connection with what is happening today, and renew your sense of wonder and awe at the delightfulness of God becoming human. This will warm your heart and make you smile more.

Epiphany of Our Lord/Second Week of Christmas

2–8 January 2022

Something to think and pray about each day this week:

What Ignatius calls disordered attachments can get the better of us–pride, greed, fear, perfectionism, the insatiable appetite for instant affirmation generated by social media, over-stimulation, the expectation of 24/7 availability, failure to realise we're stewards of creation and not its owners, obsession with prestige and status, the 'I have more than you' syndrome and all the other attractions that draw us away from God, ourselves and others, leaving us in a state of emotional turbulence, excitement and exhaustion.

My material possessions, my academic attainments, my successes, my income and my bank balance do not define my worth as an invaluable and unique human person. My worth is not determined by what's outside myself. The bad spirit, the enemy of my human nature, would have me believe otherwise. I'm infinitely richer than that. It's so easy to get caught up in what we think we need and desire, but in the cold light of day we see the illusions for what they are. Solidarity with one another, rather than competition with one another, is God's idea of what life is about.

Jim Maher SJ,
Pathways to a Decision with Ignatius of Loyola

The Presence of God

Dear Jesus, today I call on you, but not to ask for anything. I'd like only to dwell in your presence. May my heart respond to your love.

Freedom

God my creator, you gave me life and the gift of freedom. Through your love I exist in this world. May I never take the gift of life for granted. May I always respect others' right to life.

Consciousness

I ask how I am today. Am I particularly tired, stressed or anxious? If any of these characteristics apply, can I try to let go of the concerns that disturb me?

The Word

The word of God comes down to us through the Scriptures. May the Holy Spirit enlighten my mind and my heart to respond to the Gospel teachings.
(Please turn to the Scripture on the following pages. Inspiration points are there, should you need them. When you are ready, return here to continue.)

Conversation

I begin to talk with Jesus about the Scripture I have just read. What part of it strikes a chord in me? Perhaps the words of a friend–or some story I have heard recently–will rise to the surface in my consciousness. If so, does the story throw light on what the Scripture passage may be saying to me?

Conclusion

Glory be to the Father, and to the Son, and to the Holy Spirit,
As it was in the beginning, is now and ever shall be,
World without end. Amen.

Sunday 2 January
Epiphany of the Lord (USA)

Matthew 2:1–12

In the time of King Herod, after Jesus was born in Bethlehem of Judea, wise men from the East came to Jerusalem, asking, 'Where is the child who has been born king of the Jews? For we observed his star at its rising, and have come to pay him homage.' When King Herod heard this, he was frightened, and all Jerusalem with him; and calling together all the chief priests and scribes of the people, he inquired of them where the Messiah was to be born. They told him, 'In Bethlehem of Judea; for so it has been written by the prophet:

"And you, Bethlehem, in the land of Judah,
are by no means least among the rulers of Judah;
for from you shall come a ruler
who is to shepherd my people Israel."'

Then Herod secretly called for the wise men and learned from them the exact time when the star had appeared. Then he sent them to Bethlehem, saying, 'Go and search diligently for the child; and when you have found him, bring me word so that I may also go and pay him homage.' When they had heard the king, they set out; and there, ahead of them, went the star that they had seen at its rising, until it stopped over the place where the child was. When they saw that the star had stopped, they were overwhelmed with joy. On entering the house, they saw the child with Mary his mother; and they knelt down and paid him homage. Then, opening their treasure-chests, they offered him gifts of gold, frankincense, and myrrh. And having been warned in a dream not to return to Herod, they left for their own country by another road.

- The story told in today's Gospel is about people being called to follow their star in order to find the fullness of life only Jesus can give. 'I came that they may have life, and have it abundantly' (John 10:10). You may not have thought much about the nature of the star you follow. With a view to clarifying this, it may be worthwhile to ask yourself what you want for your children, your family or your friends.

Monday 3 January

Matthew 4:12–17.23–25

Now when Jesus heard that John had been arrested, he withdrew to Galilee. He left Nazareth and made his home in Capernaum by the lake, in the territory of Zebulun and Naphtali, so that what had been spoken through the prophet Isaiah might be fulfilled:

> 'Land of Zebulun, land of Naphtali,
> on the road by the sea, across the Jordan, Galilee
> of the Gentiles–

the people who sat in darkness
have seen a great light,
and for those who sat in the region and shadow
of death
light has dawned.'
From that time Jesus began to proclaim, 'Repent,
for the kingdom of heaven has come near.'

Jesus went throughout Galilee, teaching in their synagogues and proclaiming the good news of the kingdom and curing every disease and every sickness among the people. So his fame spread throughout all Syria, and they brought to him all the sick, those who were afflicted with various diseases and pains, demoniacs, epileptics, and paralytics, and he cured them. And great crowds followed him from Galilee, the Decapolis, Jerusalem, Judea, and from beyond the Jordan.

- Jesus ventures into regions where pagan influences are felt. The 'demoniacs' were in the grip of the prince of darkness: a dark shadow hung on the lives of the epileptics; and the lives of the sick were blighted also. But Jesus, Lord of light, launches the kingdom of heaven–rolling back the darkness.
- Does some dark influence also tend at times to pull me down in spirit? I open myself to the healing light of Jesus.

Tuesday 4 January

Mark 6:34–44

As he went ashore, he saw a great crowd; and he had compassion for them, because they were like sheep without a shepherd; and he began to teach them many things. When it grew late, his disciples came to him and said, 'This is a deserted place, and the hour is now very late; send them away so that they may go into the surrounding country and villages and buy something for themselves to eat.' But he answered them, 'You give them something to eat.' They said to him, 'Are we to go and buy two hundred denarii worth of bread, and give it to them to eat?' And he said to them, 'How many loaves have you? Go and see.' When they had found out, they said, 'Five, and two fish.' Then he ordered them to get all the people to sit down in groups on the green grass. So they sat down in groups of hundreds and of fifties. Taking the five loaves and the two fish, he looked up to heaven, and blessed and broke the loaves, and gave them to his disciples to set before the people; and he divided the two fish among them all. And all ate and were filled; and they took up twelve baskets full of broken pieces and of the fish. Those who had eaten the loaves numbered five thousand men.

- Out of compassion Jesus puts the people's needs first. He calls on the Twelve to share their food, to serve these thousands and then to ensure no food is wasted. Serious lessons that, with their hard hearts, they were slow to take in.

- The actions of Jesus are exactly similar to his actions at the Last Supper. Here he anticipates the superabundant gift of the Eucharist.

Wednesday 5 January

Mark 6:45–52

Immediately he made his disciples get into the boat and go on ahead to the other side, to Bethsaida, while he dismissed the crowd. After saying farewell to them, he went up on the mountain to pray.

When evening came, the boat was out on the lake, and he was alone on the land. When he saw that they were straining at the oars against an adverse wind, he came towards them early in the morning, walking on the lake. He intended to pass them by. But when they saw him walking on the lake, they thought it was a ghost and cried out; for they all saw him and were terrified. But immediately he spoke to them and said, 'Take heart, it is I; do not be afraid.' Then he got into the boat with them and the wind ceased. And they were utterly astounded, for they did not understand about the loaves, but their hearts were hardened.

- Jesus is praying–speaking with his Father. Is he perhaps thinking about the best way to 'get through' to people regarding what his coming is really about? Is he perhaps recalling the great demonstration that was his feeding of the five thousand? However, in the minds of the people, that was seen only as the beginning of a political campaign. And the disciples were little better. So now he is about to intervene on a different level: he saves the disciples from the storm to show that he is strong enough for his 'cause' to succeed without having to rely on the popular mood.

- Jesus is strong enough to carry out his plan for my life without having to rely on people who 'have influence'.

Thursday 6 January
The Epiphany of the Lord (IRE)–see entry for Sunday 2 January

Luke 4:14–22

Then Jesus, filled with the power of the Spirit, returned to Galilee, and a report about him spread through all the surrounding country. He began to teach in their synagogues and was praised by everyone.

When he came to Nazareth, where he had been brought up, he went to the synagogue on the sabbath day, as was his custom. He stood up to read, and the scroll of the prophet Isaiah was given to him. He unrolled the scroll and found the place where it was written:

'The Spirit of the Lord is upon me,
because he has anointed me
to bring good news to the poor.

He has sent me to proclaim release to the captives
and recovery of sight to the blind,
to let the oppressed go free,
to proclaim the year of the Lord's favour.'

And he rolled up the scroll, gave it back to the attendant, and sat down. The eyes of all in the synagogue were fixed on him. Then he began to say to them, 'Today this scripture has been fulfilled in your hearing.' All spoke well of him and were amazed at the gracious words that came from his mouth. They said, 'Is not this Joseph's son?'

- In my imagination I join the synagogue congregation and hear this charismatic young man speaking the prophecy of Isaiah as his own mission statement. As I listen, I sense with excitement that he is reaching out to me to join him. Lord, let me be part of that unending mission, to bring good news, vision and freedom to those who need them.

Friday 7 January

Luke 5:12–16

Once, when he was in one of the cities, there was a man covered with leprosy. When he saw Jesus, he bowed with his face to the ground and begged him, 'Lord, if you choose, you can make me clean.' Then Jesus stretched out his hand, touched him, and said, 'I do choose. Be made clean.' Immediately the leprosy left him. And he ordered him to tell no one. 'Go', he said, 'and show yourself to the priest, and, as Moses commanded, make an offering for your cleansing, for a testimony to them.' But now more than ever the word about Jesus spread abroad; many crowds would gather to hear him and to be cured of their diseases. But he would withdraw to deserted places and pray.

- I am walking along happily with Jesus and his four new fishermen disciples. I draw back in horror when this man covered with repulsive sores begs for healing. No Jew would defile himself by touching a leper, but goodness flows out of Jesus and he cures him. He orders the man to observe the command of Moses.
- Jesus is uncomfortable with all the fuss and finds a quiet place where he can be alone with his Father. Have I tried silent communion with the Lord, with maybe a phrase or a single word like 'Thanks' to help focus my attention?

Saturday 8 January

John 3:22–30

After this Jesus and his disciples went into the Judean countryside, and he spent some time there with them and baptised. John also was baptising at Aenon near Salim because water was abundant there; and people kept coming and were being baptised–John, of course, had not yet been thrown into prison.

Now a discussion about purification arose between John's disciples and a Jew. They came to John and said to him, 'Rabbi, the one who was with you across the Jordan, to whom you testified, here he is baptising, and all are going to him.' John answered, 'No one can receive anything except what has been given from heaven. You yourselves are my witnesses that I said, "I am not the Messiah, but I have been sent ahead of him." He who has the bride is the bridegroom. The friend of the bridegroom, who stands and hears him, rejoices greatly at the bridegroom's voice. For this reason my joy has been fulfilled. He must increase, but I must decrease.'

- My question as I grow older is not: 'Am I qualified enough to show Jesus to people?' More and more it is: 'Am I weak enough?' Do I accept my failures and the wounds of life as more important than my strengths in witnessing to Jesus? I am a wounded healer. Like my fellow human beings, I too am searching and struggling.

An Advent Retreat

Welcome to this year's Advent Retreat. This has been a challenging and often difficult year. We've spent some of 2021 physically apart, both from those we love and from all the familiar landmarks of our working lives, our wider relationships and the normal rhythms that give a pattern of familiarity to our daily living. A retreat in Advent helps us look forward to Christmas and a new year, but it's also an opportunity to look back reflectively on how the past year has been for us, what we've endured but also what we've learned, how we've coped and, hopefully, how we've grown and adapted.

In Luke's Gospel Simeon prophesies to Mary and Joseph in the Temple that their child 'is destined for the falling and rising of many in Israel'. He will be a sign of contradiction, 'so that the inner thoughts of many will be revealed' (Luke 2:34–35). Later in the same Gospel Jesus tells the crowd, 'Nothing is covered up that will not be uncovered, and nothing secret that will not become known' (Luke 12:2). The pandemic has revealed the vulnerability and, at times, the hypocrisy of many of the systems on which our societies depend. In personal terms it has also revealed to us hidden weaknesses and hidden strengths, opening us up to the fragility of life but also to the kindness of strangers.

This retreat is the perfect opportunity to spend some time in the presence of a loving God who is waiting to welcome us, nurture us, and draw us into deeper relationship. The Incarnation shows how it was vital to God's plan for him to draw near to us in the flesh as God-with-us. In this second year of the pandemic, we meditate on God's choice to make his love known and to give us strength in the Word made flesh.

Session 1

God With Us

Invitation to Stillness

We usually prepare for an important meeting or conversation by focusing our mind and body so that we can be fully present. At the beginning of each session we will suggest a stillness exercise and lead you through it. We begin today by inviting you to notice your breathing, the rhythm of it, and the feel and sound of each breath as you inhale and exhale. With each in-breath, allow yourself to focus on the here and now. With each out-breath, let go of any tension or concern you may feel other than being here, still, in this space. John's Gospel tells us that God is with us. God is here now, waiting to fill you with grace and peace.

Reading

John 1:1–14

In the beginning was the Word, and the Word was with God, and the Word was God. He was in the beginning with God. All things came into being through him, and without him not one thing came into being. What has come into being in him was life, and the life was the light of all people. The light shines in the darkness, and the darkness did not overcome it. The true light, which enlightens everyone, was coming into the world. He was in the world, and the world came into being through him; yet the world did not know him. He came to what was his own, and his own people did not accept him. But to all who received him, who believed in his name, he gave power to become children of God. And the Word became flesh and lived among us, and we have seen his glory, the glory as of a Father's only son, full of grace and truth.

Reflect

- During the pandemic, many of us have found ourselves distanced from the things that anchor us to who we are, or thought we were. Familiar patterns of life have changed: in our relationships, our work and our leisure. Who or what gives us a sense of who we are in such times? Who can break through the loneliness and isolation, the anxiety and the uncertainty? The name *Emmanuel* means God is with us. That's who God is: the one who is always with us, the God who is near to us, no matter what. Nothing can separate us from the love of God in Christ Jesus.
- John tells us that, from the very beginning, God's deepest nature and identity is to be word, life and light. This is who God is, and God wants to share that nature and identity with us. God wants to speak, to be in relationship with us. God wants to breathe life into us and into the whole of creation. God is

in my life and God *is* my life. There is no darkness in God. Nothing in my life or in the world can ever be stronger than God's love, shining through Jesus. Anyone who accepts the Word made flesh receives power to become the child of a God who is patient and gracious, waiting for us to accept the gift of grace and truth, offered freely and without condition.

- The prologue to John's Gospel tells us that we have a choice: to accept the Word made flesh or not. All the stories we hear during Advent show God offering the gift of his presence. Mary, Joseph, Zechariah and Elizabeth, wise men and shepherds, kings and innkeepers, all receive the same offer. In the face of the unfamiliar we can open ourselves to the God of surprises or fall silent, reject the opportunity as threat or embrace it as gift. The choice is ours.

Talk to God

- How do I feel as I hear the Gospel speak of God's plan to share our human life from the inside? How do I react to the thought of God's light shining in the darkness? There's been a lot of uncertainty and anxiety around this year. Perhaps I've been feeling 'in the dark'. This retreat is an opportunity to share with God how that darkness has felt for me. Has anything 'come to light' that I hadn't noticed before–about me, about my life and relationships, about the world around me? I take some time to savour the words: 'light shines in darkness, and darkness could not overpower it'.

- I listen again to these words: 'He was in the world that had come into being through him, and the world did not recognise him. He came to his own and his own people did not accept him.' What has helped me recently to recognise and accept God, present to me in my daily life? In times of trouble it can be hard to believe that God is truly with us, that we are in God's hands, come what may. Have the difficulties of this year challenged my capacity to live in faith, hope and love? Or have I found them growing in me, despite it all?
- John tells us that 'to those who did accept him he gave power to become children of God.' What does it mean to me to be given that power? I turn my thoughts to the many people on whom I depend: my family and friends, service workers who make my life possible, anyone I have encountered as a strength and support during the pandemic, those who have turned to me for support. What does it mean for me to see them as God's children, my brothers and sisters?
- I ask God to shine the light of grace and truth into my heart, so that I can see myself and the world around me with his merciful eyes. As I enter into Advent, I name the graces that I need and desire at this time. I spend some time quietly allowing God's word to take root and become flesh in me.

Session 2

How Can This Be?

Invitation to Stillness

As you begin this time of prayer, allow your body to settle into a peaceful and comfortable position. Let your mind settle, putting your preoccupations into God's hands for this time. Listen to the sounds around you, from those far away to those nearest to you: the sounds within your room, the sound of your own breathing, relaxing as you hear each breath drawn.

Mary listened to God's word and pondered it in her heart. Try to open your heart and mind to what God is trying to announce to you right now.

Reading

Luke 1:26–38

In the sixth month the angel Gabriel was sent by God to a town in Galilee called Nazareth, to a virgin engaged to a man whose name was Joseph, of the house of David. The virgin's name was Mary. And he came to her and said, 'Greetings, favoured one! The Lord is with you.' But she was much perplexed by his words and pondered what sort of greeting this might be. The angel said to her, 'Do not be afraid, Mary, for you have found favour with God. And now, you will conceive in your womb and bear a son, and you will name him Jesus. He will be great, and will be called the Son of the Most High, and the Lord God will give to him the throne of his ancestor David. He will reign over the house of Jacob for ever, and of his kingdom there will be no end.' Mary said to the angel, 'How can this be, since I am a virgin?' The angel said to her, 'The Holy Spirit will come upon you, and the power of the Most High will overshadow you; therefore the child to be born will be holy; he will be called Son of God. And now, your relative Elizabeth in her old age has also conceived a son; and this is the sixth month for her who was said to be barren. For nothing will be impossible with God.' Then Mary said, 'Here am I, the servant of the Lord; let it be with me according to your word.' Then the angel departed from her.

Reflect

- It's not easy to imagine the Annunciation. We don't know for certain what happened or how Mary experienced God's extraordinary communication. Medieval paintings are beautiful but often depict an exalted event, far from the mess and chaos of human reality. If Mary was at home, the domestic setting would be simple and cluttered, full of the banal, everyday features of life in a humble environment. Perhaps she saw the solid figure of an angel, or perhaps this happened in a dream. Perhaps it began as an inner whisper that gathered and grew into something clear and unmistakable. What we do know is that Mary's first reaction was to ask questions: How can this be? Why me? How can I be sure? How will I manage? These are questions many of us have grappled with at crossroad moments in our lives.

- As a woman Mary has little or no value in her society except in relation to someone else. Yet on her response hangs the fate of the whole human race. She feels uncertain, inadequate to the task, confused. But she also has faith in God, a generous heart, and is willing to take risks and go forward in trust that God will be with her.
- In Mary, God-with-us will come to life, if only she will allow this to happen. God knows her fears and waits patiently for her to make the choice. God knows what is in our deepest heart–better than we know it ourselves. God's way of dealing with us is through collaboration, not dictatorship. Knowing our hesitations, doubts and fears, God waits in both the crucial and the trivial moments of our lives for us to say yes.

Talk to God

- Has there been a sense for me, this year, of something wanting to come to birth? This has been an uncertain time, with many unusual demands on us as we adjust to a 'new normal'. Perhaps there has been a sense of loss, of the death of what felt safe and familiar. Have I been able to share this with God, allowing myself the vulnerability of mourning, or have I turned in on myself, relying on my own resources?

- If there has been loss and threat, perhaps there has also been a sense of opportunity, of new pathways opening up. The pandemic invites us to a new solidarity with the poor and the marginalised, with everything that is fragile in our world. What strengths and graces have I felt I needed to respond to the world as it is now? I ask God to widen my horizons, to give me the strength of mind and heart to see where this new way of being me in the world may lead.
- The word *angel* means messenger. What messages from God am I hearing right now? What kind of messenger am I able to be to those around me? I can be good news or bad news–the choice is mine. I spend some time with God, listening as deeply as I can to what God is announcing to me.

Session 3

Do Not Be Afraid

Invitation to Stillness

As you come into God's presence, know that God is already here, waiting for you. Allow yourself to let go of any tensions you may be carrying in your body, allowing the muscles to relax from your head, neck and face, all down your spine and lower body to your feet. Let the stillness take over and lead you to a space where you can make room for the God of dreams to be with you.

Reading

Joel 2:21–3:2

Do not fear, O soil; be glad and rejoice, for the Lord has done great things!
Do not fear, you animals of the field, for the pastures of the wilderness are green;
the tree bears its fruit, the fig tree and vine give their full yield.
O children of Zion, be glad and rejoice in the Lord your God;
for he has given the early rain for your vindication,
he has poured down for you abundant rain, the early and the later rain, as before.

The threshing-floors shall be full of grain, the vats shall overflow with wine and oil.
I will repay you for the years that the swarming locust has eaten,
the hopper, the destroyer, and the cutter, my great army, which I sent against you.
You shall eat in plenty and be satisfied, and praise the name of the Lord your God,
who has dealt wondrously with you. And my people shall never again be put to shame.
You shall know that I am in the midst of Israel, and that I, the Lord, am your God and there is no other.
And my people shall never again be put to shame.
I will pour out my spirit on all flesh; your sons and your daughters shall prophesy,
your old men shall dream dreams, and your young men shall see visions.
Even on the male and female slaves, in those days, I will pour out my spirit.

Reflect

- The Joseph of the Old Testament, Joseph with the coat of many colours, was called The Dreamer by his brothers, and they didn't mean it kindly! They didn't need people of vision–they needed people who could be realistic about the problems facing them. Joseph the carpenter of Nazareth is also portrayed as a man of dreams, but his dreams are nightmares. Mary, the love of his life, appears to have shamed and betrayed him. His dreams of love, marriage, a home and family are shattered. But in his dream he is told by the angel, 'Don't be afraid'. The same greeting as for Mary, the same invitation to a leap of faith, hope and love.

- In Joel's prophecy, old men dream dreams and young men see visions. Medieval art often portrays Joseph as an old man, beyond the longings of romantic love, but we don't know how old he actually was. If he was a young man he would have had hopes of fruitfulness–the 'quiver full' of children promised as a blessing in the Psalms–but now he feels cheated, empty and barren, without hope for the future.
- But the prophecy promises overflowing fruitfulness as God's Spirit overshadows the whole earth–not just the insiders, those who belong to the Covenant, but also outsiders and rejects, the slaves on the margins of society. God's Spirit doesn't bring only human beings to life but the soil and the animals as well–everything is brought to fulfilment in this great promise of the Day of the Lord. The angel reassures Joseph: it's good to be a dreamer, take Mary as your wife, follow your heart, for the dream you share is God's dream for the whole of creation, made flesh in the Incarnation.

Talk to God

- I let the words of Joel's prophecy sink into my heart and mind. Perhaps one phrase or word has struck me and I take time to savour it, allowing God to touch my heart. Advent is a time to reflect on God's promised gifts of grace and truth. What graces do I want to ask for right now? What truth do I want to understand and live more deeply?
- Perhaps I've had disappointments, as Joseph did. The pandemic brought many hopes and dreams to nothing, putting life on hold and limiting our choices. The disappointed disciples on the road to Emmaus had lost hope, saying to Jesus, 'We had hoped … '. Can I share with God any hopes or dreams that have been frustrated, and what that feels like?
- God also invites us in this Advent time to enter deeply into his dream for the whole of creation. Pope Francis speaks of God calling us to live together as sisters and brothers, filling the earth and making known the values of goodness, love and peace. All creation will enjoy the fruits of this promise, which appears in the prologue of John's Gospel. Those who accept Jesus into their lives will become children of God. How does it feel to be filled with the hope of that promise?
- I take time to talk to God of any disappointments or hopes that come to mind, putting all my dreams for the world into the hands of our loving Creator.

Session 4

Going Home by Another Way

Invitation to Stillness

As you come into this time of prayer, allow your senses to lead you into stillness. What can you hear beyond the music? Can you hear the sounds outside and inside where you are? Perhaps there is a scent from a candle, the freshness of the cool air, or of rain, the feel of warmth against the cold outside. Let your senses draw you into the present moment and the presence of our Creator.

Reading

Matthew 2:9–12

When they had heard the king, they set out; and there, ahead of them, went the star that they had seen at its rising, until it stopped over the place where the child was. When they saw that the star had stopped, they were overwhelmed with joy. On entering the house, they saw the child with Mary his mother; and they knelt down and paid him homage. Then, opening their treasure-chests, they offered him gifts of gold, frankincense, and myrrh. And having been warned in a dream not to return to Herod, they left for their own country by another road.

Reflect

- We talk of 'seeing stars' when we've had a knock on the head that makes us dizzy. That kind of experience leaves us feeling out of kilter, knocked off balance. Perhaps this is how the wise men felt. They were used to controlling what they saw and felt; the stars were a source of wisdom, guiding them by well-known rules. Yet suddenly here is a star that doesn't behave in the normal way, and here is an experience that confounds all their expectations.
- The mysterious, all-powerful God is born in poverty, far from royal palaces and the corridors of power. Thc wisc men bring with them treasures, symbols of the power of wealth and status, knowledge and wisdom, life and death. Yet they lay them at the feet of a newborn baby, born of a humble mother, watched over by a carpenter and some wandering shepherds. Nothing is as predicted.
- What they meet in Bethlehem is the God of surprises, the wild and unpredictable God who can never be tamed or domesticated. This is God who calls us to go home 'by another way'. Maybe we've got used to the well-worn path. Not everyone likes surprises, and we may have let ourselves get comfortable and complacent, hanging on to our safety belts. And here is God calling us out of ourselves:

step out of your comfort zone, take a walk on the wild side …

- As he grew older Jesus called many people to step off the familiar path. He called Samaritans and Jews, priest and prostitutes, Levites and lepers to become members of one family, united in love and service of one another. This is what it means to accept him into our lives and become children of God. We come home to God by God's path, not our own. We make the path by walking in faith and trust, with open minds and hearts.

Talk to God

- What is the star by which I have navigated my life's journey? What are the things that I have relied on to help me feel safe and secure, well settled in my own place? Perhaps this year has made me hold on even tighter to my securities–it's been a precarious year with danger all around us. But perhaps there has been another call, a still, small voice inviting me to live other choices and different relationships. Can I listen to that voice now, in the silence?
- What are the treasures of my life? Jesus says, 'Where your treasure is, there will your heart be also'. What gives me a sense of power and status? What makes me feel fragile and vulnerable? As I take time to be still, can I share with God my desires and anxieties,

my dreads and my dreams? Do I have a sense of God offering me gifts right now?

- I sit quietly with Jesus, sleeping in his mother's arms. What do I want to say to him, to her? Perhaps I want to hold him, the child of promise, my guiding star. Or perhaps I don't feel worthy to touch him. Can I allow God, the Word made Flesh, to touch me?

Session 5

A Future Full of Hope

Invitation to Stillness

I come to this time of quiet prayer with a desire to be still and present to God. Perhaps my mind is racing, perhaps this feels like wasted time, when life is so busy. But I offer God the gift of this time and allow the minutes to flow by, without measuring or counting. Breathing in and out, I allow myself to rest in the moment.

Reading

Matthew 2:13–21

Now after [the wise men] had left, an angel of the Lord appeared to Joseph in a dream and said, 'Get up, take the child and his mother, and flee to Egypt, and remain there until I tell you; for Herod is about to search for the child, to destroy him.' Then Joseph got up, took the child and his mother by night, and went to Egypt, and remained there until the death of Herod. This was to fulfil what had been spoken by the Lord through the prophet, 'Out of Egypt I have called my son.'

When Herod saw that he had been tricked by the wise men, he was infuriated, and he sent and killed all the children in and around Bethlehem who were two years old or under, according to the time that he had learned from the wise men. Then was fulfilled what had been spoken through the prophet Jeremiah:

> 'A voice was heard in Ramah,
> wailing and loud lamentation,
> Rachel weeping for her children;
> she refused to be consoled, because they are no more.'

When Herod died, an angel of the Lord suddenly appeared in a dream to Joseph in Egypt and said, 'Get up, take the child and his mother, and go to the land of Israel, for those who were seeking the child's life are dead.' Then Joseph got up, took the child and his mother, and went to the land of Israel.

Reflect

- This is hardly a happy Christmas scene: refugees fleeing amid terror and destruction, children murdered by an oppressive ruler, homelessness and desolate mourning. Matthew's Gospel tells of Rachel weeping for her children and refusing to be comforted. But this quotation from Jeremiah is a prophecy full of joy, hope and consolation. God says: 'Keep your voice from weeping, and your eyes from tears, for there is a reward for your work … there is hope for your future'.
- Every day our newspapers are full of violence and destruction, cruelty and death, racism and

oppression of many kinds. It would be easy to despair, especially as we face an uncertain future. But in the midst of all this, God is with us, offering us a future full of hope. We ourselves can be part of that hope for the future of the world.

- If we allow ourselves to be led by the way of Jesus, sharing the faith and courage of Joseph and Mary, the trust of the shepherds and wise men, the welcome of Elizabeth and all the familiar figures of the Nativity, we will find ourselves making real the story of Christ's birth. This is the true Christmas present–God's gift to us, but also our gift to God.
- Christmas songs and carols sing of us wanting to bring a gift to Jesus in the manger. What can we bring but our willingness to have our hearts transformed by the wonderful generosity of God? God wants nothing more from us than that willingness so that his dream of being God with us can be fulfilled.

Talk to God

- The Christmas story is full of journeys, both physical and spiritual. No one involved in the story of the Incarnation is left in the same place that they started from. God's invitation waits for our response, but never leaves us standing. I may find myself shying away from the harder parts of the story–this is not the safe and happy Christmas of childhood. How do I react to the harsher parts of the narrative, where nothing feels safe or stable? I take time to get into the minds of Joseph and Mary as they pack up and escape, with horror following behind them. Perhaps I talk to them or share in their conversation with each other. What does it feel like, to try and keep faith and hope alive in such a situation? What do I find myself wanting to say to God?

- Jesus is so small and vulnerable. He escapes, while others die. I allow my thoughts to dwell on the many refugees and terrified children, the desperate families on our own borders right now, trying to find shelter and a new life. Have these Advent meditations changed the way I think of them? How do I see God with us in them?
- Finally, I sit quietly and allow God to speak to me through the scriptures. Perhaps I can take time to find Jeremiah's prophecy and share in Rachel's joy, despite her weeping and desolation. How do these scripture passages speak to me in times of joy or of sadness? Are there joys and sorrows I want to share with God right now? Joseph is presented as a model of obedience, a word that means to listen attentively. How am I being called in my own life to listen attentively to God's promises?

Conclusion

As our Advent Retreat ends, it may be helpful to spend some time reflecting on the process as a whole. Has this time of prayerful pondering on God's word moved your heart in any way or led you to think differently about the entry into human life of God-with-us? Is there a scripture passage or word that has become special to you? In what way have you encountered God-with-you in the events of your life or in the world around you? There are many practical as well as spiritual implications to the Christmas story. Did you find yourself struggling at any point, or resisting the words and meaning of the scriptures you read? You may find it helpful to look back at any insights you received or any sense of invitation to respond to God's word. Has anything emerged that needs healing or transformation? Has there been a sense of growth in courage to move something forward or forge a new path? Where might God be leading you home 'by another way'? The Christmas story is one of surprises, and of people allowing God into their lives in unexpected ways. Above all it's a story of obedience, of people listening attentively to God's dream and sharing it in their own way, each according to their capacity. Take some time to explore any sense you have had of grace being offered, to ask for the courage to respond, and to thank God for every gift: those recognised and acted upon, and those yet to be understood and realised. Perhaps you can offer God the Christmas gift of your time and attention in the days to come as you continue on the road to Bethlehem with Jesus Emmanuel, God-with-us.

> O Wisdom … Lord and ruler … Root of Jesse … Key of David … Rising Sun … King of the Nations … Emmanuel … Come, Lord Jesus.